RACIAL D[...]ON:
17 YEARS [...]CT

G000128146

Colin Brown
Pat Gay

No. 646

ISBN No. 0-85374-264-2

Published by Policy Studies Institute
100 Park Village East, London NW1 3SR
Printed by Bourne Offset Ltd.

Preface

This reseach project was conducted by the Policy Studies Institute in collaboration with the Commission for Racial Equality. The funding for the work was provided by the Commission for Racial Equality.

This report on the study as a whole will be followed by reports on each of the three cities covered by the research: London, Birmingham and Manchester. These reports will be published by the Commission for Racial Equality and will also contain statistics concerning the local labour markets and the position of black people within them.

Acknowledgements

Jim Hubbuck at the Commission for Racial Equality was a joint manager of the project and gave us valuable help at all stages of the work. David Smith at PSI also gave us advice and help throughout the study.

The pilot fieldwork for the project was carried out by Sheila Benson and Stephen Small at PSI; they established many of the detailed procedures on which the main fieldwork was based.

The study would have been impossible without the goodwill and hard work of many people who typed letters, forwarded letters, made phone calls, and helped us to contact the right people at the right times. In London, our personal thanks go to Dhirendra, Jheni, Pam, Raj, Ray, Safder, Stephanie and Thelma; in Birmingham, to Alison, Dean, Geoff, Joy, Leroy, Mohammed Javed, Nassim, Pat, Raghib, Ron, Satnam and Steve; in Manchester, to Angela, Brian, Carol, Fiona (and her colleagues), Jack, Kaleem, Pat, Si, Suchi and Winston.

CONTENTS

LIST OF TABLES

I Introduction

Racial discrimination in employment

In 1968 the British Parliament passed legislation that for the first time made it unlawful for employers to discriminate between job applicants on grounds of racial origin. The 1968 Race Relations Act came into force in November of that year. The law was consolidated and extended in the 1976 Race Relations Act. Racial discrimination in recruitment has therefore been outlawed in this country for nearly 17 years.

The main aims of this report are to give a minimum estimate of how extensive discrimination is today and, by making comparisons with previous research, to show trends in the extent of discrimination over the past ten years.

The following extracts from the 1976 Race Relations Act set out the basic legal obligation of employers to deal fairly with applicants from different racial backgrounds:

'A person discriminates against another in any circumstances relevant for the purposes of any provision of this Act if -

(a) on racial grounds he treats that other less favourably than he treats or would treat other persons; or

(b) he applies to that other a requirement or condition which he applies or would apply equally to persons not of the same racial group as that other but -

    i) which is such that the proportion of persons of the same racial group as that other who can comply with it is considerably smaller than the proportion of persons not of that racial group who can comply with it; and

    (ii) which he cannot show to be justifiable irrespective of the colour, race, nationality or ethnic or national origins of the person to whom it is applied; and

1

(iii)   which is to the detriment of that other because he cannot comply with it...'

'... It is unlawful for a person, in relation to employment by him at an establishment in Great Britain, to discriminate against another -
(a)   in the arrangements he makes for the purpose of determining who should be offered that employment; or
(b)   in the terms on which he offers him that employment; or
(c)   by refusing or deliberately omitting to offer him that employment.'

It is important to understand that the law makes a distinction between those acts of <u>direct</u> discrimination where a job applicant is selected or rejected by an employer simply and deliberately on the basis of his or her racial origin, and those acts best described as <u>indirect</u> discrimination, where practices and policies racially bias the recruitment process, regardless of the way they are formulated and regardless of the employer's motive. The research described in this report provides a measure of the extent of direct discrimination only; it provides no measure of the extent to which black people are further disadvantaged in the job market by indirect discrimination.

A minimum measure
The method used to estimate the level of direct discrimination faced by black job applicants is one used by different researchers in several countries over the past 19 years. The essence of the 'discrimination test' (or 'situation test' as it has also been called) is the recording of the responses of individuals and organisations advertising job vacancies when approached by applicants of differing ethnic origins. This is done experimentally by employing actors or by making bogus written applications; the individuals and organisations under study have no knowledge of the experiment. Applications are taken no further than an initial request for an interview, and, whilst the experiments reveal the extent of direct discrimination at this first contact, no information is obtained on any discrimination that might occur at later stages of the recruitment process. This is why we refer to the result of the tests as a minimum measure of the extent of discrimination; when genuine applicants for jobs surmount the first obstacle of obtaining an interview, they may still be treated unfairly on the grounds of race at the interview or during the actual selection of the successful

2

applicant. It is therefore likely that the actual level of direct discrimination faced by black job applicants is greater than is reported here.

Previous measurements of discrimination

The first research of this type was published in 1967 by one of PSI's predecessor institutes, Political and Economic Planning (PEP). Since then the method has been used several times in Britain, and there have been similar studies in the USA, the Netherlands, France and Australia. Most of the work has concerned employment recruitment, but tests have also been conducted with estate agents, private landlords, insurance companies and car hire firms. References to all these studies are given at the end of this report, but we describe below the two that are of greatest interest. These are the sets of tests carried out by PEP in 1973-4 and by the Nottingham Community Relations Council between 1977 and 1979, and it is their results that are used later in this report to try to understand the changes in the level of discrimination over the past ten years.

The PEP study comprised a series of tests in six towns and cities in England to assess the discrimination faced by people of West Indian, Indian, Pakistani, Italian and Greek origins when trying to obtain jobs, buy houses and obtain private tenancies(1). The applications were made personally or by letter, as appropriate. The employment tests covered a broad range of jobs from unskilled manual work to accountancy, and revealed that there was considerable discrimination against the black applicants. For each job a pair of applications were made, one by a white person and one by someone of a different ethnic origin. One third of the employers rejected the black applicants while offering to take the white applications further. Part of the research design was a comparison of the effect of being an immigrant and the effect of being black: the much lower level of discrimination faced by the Greek and Italian applicants (about one case in ten) showed that discrimination was more related to race than to overseas origin. Comparisons between the results of the tests using West Indian, Indian and Pakistani applicants showed that there was no significant difference between the levels of discrimination faced by the various black groups.

In Nottingham between 1977 and 1979 the local Community Relations Council (CRC) conducted a similar set of tests for non-manual jobs advertised in that city. For each vacancy three written applications were made, one by a white person, one by a person of West Indian origin and one by a person of Asian origin.

The results showed that the level of discrimination faced by blacks in Nottingham was even higher than that found in the PEP study: over forty per cent of employers rejected the black applicants while offering the white applicant an interview(2).

II The Tests

At the heart of the discrimination test method is the experimental comparison of an employer's reactions to applicants with different ethnic origins but with equivalent qualifications for the job. Although the principle is simple, the need to control those factors that could bias the results does make the execution of the tests fairly complicated. In the next few pages we explain in some detail the way in which the tests were carried out.

The three-applicant test
The two studies described earlier did not share exactly the same research methods. The PEP tests employed a pair of applicants for each job, one of whom was white and the other of a different ethnic origin. The Nottingham CRC tests employed three applicants for each job: one white, one of West Indian origin and one of Asian origin. Although the three-applicant test is correspondingly more expensive to administer for each vacancy, it is more valuable than the two-applicant test because it gives an indication of any tendency on the part of individual employers to treat Asian and West Indian applicants differently. For this reason it was decided to use three-applicant tests in the present study.

When we compare the results of this project with those of the PEP and the Nottingham CRC projects it is necessary to employ a statistical approach that is different from the one used in reporting the main findings: this modified treatment is required because of the move from the two-applicant test to the three-applicant test, and is fully explained later.

Valid and invalid tests
Where one or more applicant is invited by the employer to take their application further the results are, for our purposes, fairly easy to classify: the employer treats the applicants equally favourably or one is favoured above another. However, in cases where all

of the applicants are rejected, things are not so simple. In a sense they have all been treated equally, but in fact we have no evidence as to whether discrimination has taken place. The applications may have been turned down for a number of reasons: an earlier applicant may have got the job, or there may have been a better-qualified applicant, or the researcher's assessment of the kinds of qualifications required may have been wrong. Had each of the test applicants been better qualified, or had they applied sooner, then the employer would have had the opportunity to discriminate. There is a logical asymmetry between the equal treatment of success and the equal treatment of failure. For this reason we accepted as valid only the tests where one or more applicant received a positive response; where all three applicants were rejected, the test was treated as invalid. This is the practice adopted by the PEP and Nottingham CRC studies.

This procedure also makes sense if the problem is viewed in mathematical terms. The previous studies of this kind have shown that as the labour market changes, so the proportion of all-negative test results fluctuates, simply because when there are fewer vacancies there are more applicants for each one and a higher proportion are rejected at the first stage of selection. This fluctuation is quite wide - in this study nearly half of the letter test results were all-negative, but in Jowell and Prescott-Clarke's study, carried out in 1969 when unemployment was very much lower, only one in six tests gave the corresponding result. If the all-negative results were treated as valid cases of equal, non-discriminatory treatment, then the test results would automatically show a decrease in the level of discrimination every time jobs became scarce, and an increase in discrimination when jobs became more plentiful, irrespective of the true level of discrimination. Inclusion of the all-negative results would therefore make the tests statistically worthless for detecting change over time, as they would in fact be a more sensitive indicator of changes in the number of applicants for each job than of changes in the extent of racial discrimination.

The three areas
The tests were carried out in London, Birmingham and Manchester, with roughly a third of the work in each area. It was agreed to concentrate on these three cities for several reasons.

First, it was not possible to cover a sample of vacancies that would be nationally representative (as, for instance, in the case of a national interview survey) because of the costs that would have been involved. The three urban areas around the cities chosen

6

contain some 60 per cent of Britain's black population, and are therefore the areas that give the best coverage of the geographical labour markets in which black workers find themselves. Secondly, within the size of the project, statistically reliable results can be derived for each of the areas separately: the project involved tests with over a hundred employers in each area. Whilst it is useful to have results that have validity for the whole sample of tests, it is also important to have results that stand up separately within each of the areas included in that sample. Had the same total number of tests been spread thinner, over a larger number of towns and cities, the statistical reliability of the results from each individual area would have been at risk. Thirdly, the areas chosen have different types of labour market, and in particular have different levels of unemployment. This gives a good spread of conditions in which to carry out the tests in order to avoid the possibility that the estimated extent of racial discrimination was peculiar to a single set of circumstances. In the GLC area in July 1984 the overall official level of unemployment was 10.0 per cent, while it was 15.8 per cent in the West Midlands Metropolitan County and 14.4 per cent in the Greater Manchester Metropolitan County. It was also hoped that any differences in the results might illuminate the relationship between changes in the unemployment rate and the extent of racial discrimination.

Practical considerations meant that we had to choose parts of London, rather than the Greater London area as a whole, in which to carry out the tests. We chose Croydon, central London, and Islington as representing a range of local job markets. In Birmingham and Manchester the much smaller geographical size of the cities meant that we were able to apply for any jobs advertised in the local papers, with the proviso that they were not completely unreasonable travelling distances from the applicants' addresses. The test applicants had addresses near to each other, to ensure that differences in travel-to-work distances did not affect the employer's view of their suitability for the job.

The types of job
The research aimed to cover a range of jobs in the non-manual and skilled manual fields, with an even spread between sets of male and female applicants, and a good balance between jobs for people about 30 years old and for people 18 to 20 years old. There was also some value in choosing job categories that had been used for the PEP and the Nottingham CRC tests. There were also practical considerations in the choice of jobs - vacancies had to exist in such numbers as to enable the researchers to organise sufficient applic-

ations during the lifetime of the project. Only private-sector jobs were included in the study, partly for continuity with the previous studies and partly because recruitment and selection procedures in the civil service and in local authorities are as a rule more complex than in the private sector, making the discrimination test a rather unsatisfactory method in their case. The choice of male or female applicants for the different jobs was made along the lines of traditional sex roles; to do otherwise would have introduced into the experimental design a further complicating factor, which would only have been justifiable if the tests were also aimed at assessing the extent of discrimination based on sex. To cover both race and sex discrimination within the same set of tests would require a different design and a much larger project altogether, and it was therefore agreed from the start to keep to race alone.

After a series of pilot tests and a period of checking the vacancies advertised in the newspapers, the following types of job were selected:

For tests by letter application
Sales representative, age about 30 (male applicants)
Secretary, age about 30 (female applicants)
Clerical worker, age about 30 (female applicants)
Junior sales representative, age 18-20 (male applicants)
Office junior, age 18-20 (female applicants)
Office junior, age 18-20 (male applicants)

For tests by telephone application
Skilled manual worker, age about 30 (male applicants)

In the event there were few advertised jobs in the younger age group that male applicants could write in for. Over the period of the study only eight valid junior sales representative tests were completed, and there was not a single office junior vacancy for which we obtained a valid test for males. As a consequence of these difficulties, there are no male office junior results, and the junior sales representative results have been combined with the older sales representative results. We had expected these junior vacancies to be less common than the others, but were unprepared to find that this part of the job market was almost non-existent, at least as regards newspaper advertisements.

Most of the vacancies were found in the local newspapers, although a few were advertised in the national press. Sometimes the applicant had to write to an address outside their city; in all of these cases, however, the actual job was to work within that city or the work covered the city within a regional sales area.

8

The letter tests

Applications for the non-manual vacancies were prepared by the PSI researchers, but the addresses used for the 'applicants' were those of volunteers. In each area all three were located in districts that were known to have relatively large numbers of black residents. The volunteers received the replies and sent them on to PSI after cancelling any interviews that were offered by the employers. All of the applicants' names were fictitious.

The ethnic origin of the West Indian applicant was indicated by stating that their early education was in Jamaica, and with a distinctive name; the Asian applicant had a distinctive Hindu name.

Every effort was made to ensure that the three applicants had equivalent experience and qualifications and that the employer would see them as independent applications. Special measures adopted were as follows:

- Three basic letter-types were used for each job, and these were rotated between the three applicants between each vacancy within each job category. Only the details pertaining to each specific vacancy were altered. Examples of the letter types are given in an appendix to this report.

- The three letter types were prepared with word processors using different 'daisy-wheel' typefaces (to simulate different typewriters), and different layouts. Each was on a different size and colour of paper and was put in a matching envelope. All of these features were rotated. The three signatures were in different handwriting, and used different inks, but all were clear and neat.

- For the junior applicants a small error was deliberately introduced in each. In one, a spurious full stop was inserted and removed with typist's correcting fluid; in another, there was an indenting error on one paragraph; the third letter was set too high on the page. These 'errors' were rotated between each vacancy.

- All the letters were posted on the same morning or afternoon, in different postboxes in the city. All had first-class stamps. Addresses on the envelopes were all written in the same hand as the signature on the letter or were all typed in the same typeface and style as the letter.

- The qualifications and previous jobs that were filled in by

9

the researcher were carefully chosen to be equivalent but not identical. Where possible, the same sets of three were used in rotation for similar jobs. In individual cases where it was felt one set of qualifications was slightly better than the others, and it was unavoidable, then the better set was given to one of the black applicants. This ensured that if there was any bias caused by the choice of qualifications it would lower, rather than raise, the estimate of the extent of discrimination.

The basic qualifications and experience are set out in the standard letters shown in the appendix. In each case the researcher added the details of the applicant's present post.

Evaluation of the replies was made according to a simple set of rules. A positive response was recorded when the employer replied offering an interview, enclosing an application form or asking the applicant to make contact by telephone. A negative response was recorded where the employer replied but rejected the application, or when there was no reply at all.

The telephone tests

In each city three volunteers agreed to make telephone applications for the skilled manual vacancies, which are mostly advertised with telephone numbers rather than addresses. One volunteer was white, one was of West Indian origin and one was of Asian origin. Both black volunteers had ethnically distinctive accents but spoke good English and all the volunteers had a competent telephone manner. Again, precautions were taken to ensure the tests were unbiased:

- In each case, to avoid the chance of a spurious apparent case of discrimination against the black applicants, the white applicant phoned last. Thus, if the job happened to be taken by a real applicant in between our calls, or the employer decided he or she had enough applicants coming for interviews, it would only appear as discrimination against the white applicant. In two of the tests this rule was broken and the white applicant phoned first; in both cases the white tester was encouraged but one or both the black applicants were rejected, therefore to ensure that there was no mistake another white tester (one of the authors) phoned for the job and also received a positive response. All interviews were cancelled by phone after the test was complete.

- All three telephone calls were on the same afternoon.

- The applicants all gave their names as soon as the conversation started. The Asian name was a distinctive Hindu or Sikh name; the West Indian applicant also had a distinctive name, although it was expected that the employer would be most likely to identify his ethnic origin by his accent. From all of the testers' accents it was also clear that they were local residents and had working-class backgrounds.

- All three had job histories that were equivalent but not identical. These were rotated, and were altered to suit the vacancy. The qualifications were often identical but small alterations were made to give some variation (for example, all had full apprenticeships, but they were served in different firms). Employers were usually content to ask very basic questions about qualifications, and were mainly concerned with the applicant's present job.

- Before each set of calls the PSI researcher and the testers had a discussion about the job in question, to ensure all had knowledge of key facts and - most important - the necessary vocabulary to cope with any questions. Where there was no knowledge of a specific type of work within the team the vacancy was avoided.

- The PSI researcher supervised the calls and noted any factors that may have biased or invalidated the results. Several sets of results were rejected as a consequence of difficulties with one of the applications, and this was usually the result of one of the volunteers giving an answer to an employer's question that gave a much better or much worse impression than the others.

Evaluation of the responses was again made by simple rules. A positive response was recorded when the employer offered the job, offered an interview, or asked the applicant to telephone later for a discussion of the work involved. A negative response was recorded when the applicant was rejected or told to telephone later because there was no-one there to deal with the enquiry. When the testers were asked to phone back for this reason, the recall was attempted if the time given was within the test session (usually an afternoon), and in these cases it was only recorded as a negative response once the second attempt had been made.

For the letter tests, the numbers of invalid tests (those with all-negative results) could be accurately recorded, because it was always clear when all the applications received negative responses. For the telephone tests, however, it was hard to make a firm distinction between invalid tests and some of the tests abandoned for reasons of non-contact or because the applicants found themselves speaking to different people or different departments. We have therefore not calculated an exact figure for the proportion of invalid telephone tests.

Timing
The tests began in February 1984 and the majority were competed by the end of March 1985. Over 90 per cent were carried out in 1984.

III The Results

The final tally of tests is shown below. Sets of postal applications were sent to over 450 employers, and from these over 250 valid discrimination tests were obtained. Over 100 employers were telephoned by the volunteer 'applicants' and from these nearly 70 valid discrimination tests were obtained.

Table 1   Number of discrimination tests

	Number of vacancies
Valid tests	
Sales representative	91
Junior sales representative	8
Secretary	89
Clerical worker (female)	38
Office junior (female)	41
Skilled manual (telephone tests)	68
Total Valid Tests	335
Invalid letter tests	199

N.B.   It is not possible to give an accurate figure for the number of invalid telephone tests, for reasons explained in the previous chapter. Roughly speaking, just over half the telephone tests were invalid.

Joiner/carpenter	26	Spray painter	2
Bricklayer	11	Panel beater/body-worker	2
Motor mechanic/fitter	10	Painter/decorator	2
Plasterer	7	Sheet metalworker	1
Electrician	3	Toolmaker	1
Plumber	3		

As explained earlier, vacancies were more scarce for some job categories than for others, and the wide variation in the numbers of tests completed for each job type is a reflection of this.

Overall outcome of the tests
Table 2 shows, for the study as a whole and for each job type, the way the employers responded to the three applicants. In nearly half of the cases all three applicants received positive responses - that is to say they were offered interviews or sent application forms. In nearly a quarter of all the tests two applicants received positive responses while the third was rejected - although in only four per cent of all cases was this the white applicant, compared with ten per cent for the West Indian applicant and ten per cent for the Asian applicant. Nearly a third of all employers rejected two applicants although, again, the rejections were not evenly distributed between the three applicants. Most of them were rejections of both black applicants, rather than rejection of one white and one black applicant. This general pattern can be seen to be repeated for every one of the job types, with some minor variations.

This is evidence of substantial racial discrimination against both the Asian applicant and the West Indian applicant for each type of job. It also shows that although a small group of employers discriminate against black applicants of Asian origin but not against those of West Indian origin, and a further group vice-versa, the total impact of discrimination on the two black applicants is the same. This is made clearer in Table 3, where we compare the proportions of each applicant's responses that were positive. Taking all the valid tests together, we can see that 90 per cent of the white applications were successful, compared with 63 per cent of the Asian applications and the West Indian applications. The white applicant was therefore over a third more likely than either of the black applicants to receive a positive response.

Table 2   Outcome of valid tests for the different job types

	All job types	Male sales rep.	Female secretary	Female clerk	Female office junior	Male skilled manual
a) All three responses positive	46	37	51	37	37	62
b) Asian applicant rejected	10	14	10	3	10	9
c) West Indian applicant rejected	10	11	8	8	17	7
d) White applicant rejected	4	5	3	8	2	3
e) Asian and West Indian applicants rejected	25	23	24	37	29	19
f) Asian and White applicants rejected	2	4	3	3	-	-
g) West Indian and white applicants rejected	3	5	1	5	5	-
Base: Total vacancies	335	99	89	38	41	68

Note: A valid test is one where at least one of the applicants received a positive response, that is an interview or application form in the case of the letter tests, or, in the case of the telephone tests, a job, an interview or an invitation to discuss the job further.

Table 3   Outcome of applications by ethnic origin.   Valid tests only

	Total	White	Asian	West Indian
All job types				
Positive outcome	72	90	63	63
Negative outcome	28	10	37	37
Base: Total applications	1005	335	335	335
Male Sales Rep.				
Positive outcome	70	86	59	61
Negative outcome	30	14	41	39
Base: Total applications	297	99	99	99
Female Secretary				
Postive outcome	74	92	63	67
Negative outcome	26	8	37	33
Base: Total applications	267	89	89	89
Female Clerk				
Positive outcome	65	84	58	53
Negative outcome	35	16	42	47
Base: Total applications	114	38	38	38
Female Office Junior				
Positive outcome	67	93	61	49
Negative outcome	33	7	39	51
Base: Total applications	123	41	41	41
Male Skilled Manual				
Positive outcome	81	97	72	74
Negative outcome	19	3	28	26
Base: Total applications	204	68	68	68

Although the applications were designed to be equivalent to each other, they were not identical, and one would therefore expect to find that in some cases an employer would show a preference or a dislike for one of them, for reasons that have nothing to do with race. However, as the characteristics of the applicants were rotated, these cases should be distributed randomly throughout all the tests, along with other chance factors such as delays in the postal service or even variations in the efficiency of the employer's first sift through the applications. To ensure that the variations in the success rate of the three applicants could not be the result of these random variations we applied the chi-squared test of statistical significance to the figures in Table 3. The test shows that there is less than one chance in a thousand that the differences between the success rates of the white and the West Indian, or between those of the white and the Asian, are the results of random variations in the responses to their applications.

When we apply the same test to the small difference between the success rates of the two black applicants, however, we find that it is not statistically significant: in other words it is within the degree of random variation you would expect to find within these test results.

How widespread is racial discrimination?
So far we have analysed the test results in terms of the individual success rates of the three applicants; we have seen that black applicants for jobs are less likely to be successful than equally-qualified white applicants, but although this gives some idea of the overall impact of discrimination on black job-seekers it does not show the frequency with which acts of racial discrimination are taking place. For an impression of how widespread racial discrimination is we need an estimate of the proportion of employers actually committing acts of racial discrimination. Using the figures from Table 2 we can calculate a minimum estimate of this proportion.

The argument is a little complicated, because within the calculation we try to take into account the level of the random variation discussed above. Table 2 shows the percentage of employers appearing to discriminate against both black applicants - figure (e), which is 25 per cent overall; the table also shows the percentage appearing to discriminate in favour of the white applicant but against only one of the black applicants - figure (b) plus figure (c), adding to 20 per cent overall. As we have said, some of this apparent discrimination is due to minor differences between the applications and to other factors outside our control:

17

although the rotation of letter types and qualifications ensures that the impact of these factors on the overall success rates of the three applicants is equalised, this equalisation does not work at the level of the individual vacancy, and some of the apparently unfair choices made by the employers will be the consequence of these uncontrolled factors. We can calculate the range within which this error lies, and can therefore reduce the raw discrimination figures accordingly.

Because of the rotation of letter types and qualifications, we can be certain that the maximum level of this error is equivalent to the total level of discrimination against the white applicant. It is unlikely to be as high as this, but we are setting the top limit here. In theory it is possible that all of the apparent discrimination detected is actual discrimination, and therefore the bottom limit of this error is zero.

We make the calculations separately for the proportion of employers who discriminate against blacks of both Asian origin and West Indian origin and for the proportion of employers who discriminate against only one of them. The maximum level of the error in the case of discrimination against both is the average of figures (f) and (g), which is 2.5 per cent; the maximum level of the error in the case of discrimination against only one of the black applicants is figure (d), which is 4 per cent. We can now calculate the mimimum estimate of the proportion of employers discriminating in recruitment. The minimum percentage discriminating against both black applicants is equivalent to figure (e) minus its maximum level of error, that is to say 25 per cent minus 2.5 per cent; it is therefore 22.5 per cent. The mimimum percentage discriminating against only one of the black applicants is equivalent to figure (b) minus its maximum level of error, plus figure (c) minus its maximum level of error, that is to say 10 per cent minus 4 per cent, plus 10 per cent minus 4 per cent; it is therefore 12 per cent.

We now have the ranges in which, according to these tests, the 'true' proportions lie: the percentage of employers discriminating against both black applicants is between 22.5 per cent and 25 per cent; the percentage of employers discriminating against only one of the black applicants is between 12 per cent and 20 per cent; the percentage of employers discriminating against one or both black applicants is therefore between 34.5 per cent and 45 per cent. The proportion of employers who, according to these tests, discriminate against white applicants lies in the range zero to nine per cent.

As explained earlier, these test results almost certainly

understate the true extent of racial discrimination, and we are therefore aiming to give minimum estimates throughout this report. For this reason the lower figures for discrimination against black applicants calculated above are the most useful. We can say confidently that a mimimum of one in five of the employers in these job categories in these areas discriminate against both Asian and West Indian job applicants and at least a further one in eight discriminate against either Asian or West Indian applicants; in total at least a third of all the employers discriminate against one or both groups of black applicants.

Comparisons of the results for the different jobs

For every job type the comparison of the success rates of the black applicants shows a substantial level of racial discrimination, and the chi-squared tests show the differences are statistically significant at the 0.01 level in every case except one. This case is the comparison of the white and Asian success rates for the female clerical jobs (84 per cent and 58 per cent respectively) and the test gives a chi-squared value with a probability less than 0.05. None of the comparisons of the Asian and West Indian success rates are statistically significant at the 0.05 level.

Although the difference between the success rates of the white and black applicants varies from one job type to another (it is smallest for the skilled manual jobs and largest for the office junior jobs), this variation is not consistently repeated within each area, and it is not statistically significant.

In Tables 4 and 5 the results are grouped according to the applicants' sex and age groups. It can be seen from inspection that there is little difference between the results for men and women; in both cases there is a substantial level of discrimination against the black applicants and although this is slightly worse for the women the sex difference is not statistically significant. The results for younger and older applicants are also very close together and although discrimination for the younger applicants is a little worse, the gap between the age groups is not statistically significant. It should be remembered when using the figures from this table that the sex and age of the applicant in our set of tests are not independent: because we were unable to carry out any valid tests involving vacancies for male office juniors, and could only complete eight junior sales representative tests, 41 out of the 49 tests in the 18-20 age group involve female applicants. When restricted to women, the comparison shows even less difference between the two age groups.

Table 4   Outcome of valid tests for men and women, and for younger and older applicants

	All job types	Male applicants	Female applicants	Applicants aged 28-30	Applicants aged 18-20
a) All three responses positive	46	47	44	47	39
b) Asian applicant rejected	10	12	8	10	10
c) West Indian applicant rejected	10	10	10	9	16
d) White applicant rejected	4	4	4	5	2
e) Asian and West Indian applicants rejected	25	22	28	24	29
f) Asian and White applicants rejected	2	2	2	3	-
g) West Indian and White applicants rejected	3	3	3	3	4
Base: Total vacancies	335	167	168	286	49

Table 5   Outcome of applications by ethnic origin by sex and age. Valid tests only.

Column Percentages

	Total	White	Asian	West Indian
Men				
Positive outcome	73	90	64	66
Negative outcome	27	10	36	34
Base: Total applications	501	167	167	167
Women				
Positive outcome	70	90	61	59
Negative outcome	30	10	39	41
Base: Total applications	504	168	168	168
Age 28-30				
Positive outcome	72	90	63	64
Negative outcome	28	10	37	36
Base: Total applications	858	286	286	286
Age 18-20				
Positive outcome	69	94	61	51
Negative outcome	31	6	39	49
Base: Total applications	147	49	49	49

Comparison of the results for the different areas

So far we have seen that the level of discrimination is fairly consistent over the different categories of test. In Tables 6 and 7 we look at the results for the three geographical areas of the study. The first and most important point to note is that in all three the level of discrimination against the black applicants is substantial and the difference between the success rates of the black and white applicants is significant at the 0.01 probability level.

Comparisons between the three areas are complicated. The gap between the overall success rates of the black and white applicants is greatest in Birmingham and least in London. This relationship is quite strong for the letter tests, but is almost inverted in the case of the telephone tests, during which London showed by far the greatest level of discrimination. The comparisons between the areas are not statistically significant at the 0.05 level, and this is true whether all the job types are taken together or the letter tests and telephone tests are considered separately. Overall, the results are consistent with the hypothesis that discrimination is more likely to happen in areas where jobs are scarce, but the support for the theory is very weak, first because the overall relationship is not statistically significant, and secondly because all of the relationship comes from the letter tests: for the telephone tests of discrimination in recruitment to skilled manual jobs, London emerges as the worst of the three areas. Even for the letter tests taken on their own the difference between the three areas is not statistically significant. Finally, therefore, it is not possible to conclude from these tests that racial discrimination varies in any systematic way between different geographical labour markets in Britain.

Table 6   Outcome of valid tests for different conurbations

	All areas	London	Birm-ingham	Man-chester
a) All three responses positive	46	49	46	42
b) Asian applicant rejected	10	11	12	8
c) West Indian applicant rejected	10	8	6	16
d) White applicant rejected	4	6	3	4
e) Asian and West Indian applicants rejected	25	21	31	23
f) Asian and White applicants rejected	2	2	2	3
g) West Indian and White applicants rejected	3	3	1	5
Base: Total vacancies	335	121	108	106

Table 7 Outcome of applications by ethnic origin in each area. Valid tests only

Column Percentages

	Total	White	Asian	West Indian
London				
Positive outcome	74	88	66	68
Negative outcome	26	12	34	32
Base: Total applications	363	121	121	121
Birmingham				
Positive outcome	71	94	56	63
Negative outcome	29	6	44	37
Base: Total applications	324	108	108	108
Manchester				
Positive outcome	70	89	66	57
Negative outcome	30	11	34	43
Base: Total applications	318	106	106	106

IV Trends Over the Last Decade

An important aim of the study was to obtain an estimate of the extent of racial discrimination in employment recruitment that could be compared with those of the 1973/4 PEP study and the 1977/9 Nottingham CRC study. For this reason there is some continuity in the selection of the job types covered in our project and these earlier ones. The results provide no evidence to suggest that the level of racial discrimination has decreased since 1973.

The paired-test model
The present study and the Nottingham CRC study both used three-applicant tests, while the 1973/4 PEP study used two-applicant tests, and the results are therefore of a slightly different form. While our tests can have seven valid permutations of results (see Tables 2, 4 and 6) the two-applicant tests can only have three permutations: both positive, white positive but black negative, and white negative but black positive. We cannot directly compare the two sets of results. However, we can treat each three-applicant test as a pair of two-applicant tests: that is to say the Asian-white element of the test and the West Indian-white element are treated as separate tests. We refer to this as the 'paired-test' model, and it gives us two results for each employer; obviously, it does not double-up the scale of our study in terms of statistical reliability since it is still based on the same number of employers. The results of the three studies are shown in Tables 8 and 9.

Comparisons of the same jobs
The three studies have only a limited overlap in respect of job types, and Table 8 therefore gives both overall comparisons for the letter tests and comparisons based on the common job types: sales representatives, secretaries and female junior clerks ('office juniors'). For all three studies the level of apparent discrimination against the white applicant is around seven per cent. The

25

Table 8   Comparisons between tests in 1973/4, 1977/9 and 1984/5. Correspondence tests only

Column Percentages

	1973/4 PEP study		1977/9 CRE study		1984/5 PSI study	
	All jobs	Comparison group	All jobs	Comparison group	All jobs	Comparison group
No discrimination	58	64	46	44	54	56
Discrimination against black applicant	36	30	48	49	38	37
Discrimination against white applicant	6	7	6	7	8	7
Number of vacancies covered by tests	234	138	103	59	267	229

Notes: (1) The percentages for the 1977/9 and 1984/5 studes are calculated using the paired test model. See text for explanation.

(2) The job categories for the three studies are as follows:

	1973/4	1977/9	1984/5
'All jobs':	Junior clerk (M)	Junior clerk (M)	Junior clerk (F)
	Junior clerk (F)	Junior clerk (F)	Sales rep. (M)
	Salesman (M)	Shop Asst. (F)	Clerk (F)
	Accountant (M)	Salesman (M)	Secretary (F)
	Management trainee (M)	Secretary (F)	
	Secretary (F)		
'Comparison group':		Junior clerk (F)	
		Sales rep. (M)	
		Secretary (F)	

Table 9   Comparisons between tests in 1973/4, 1977/9 and
           1984/5: individual job categories

Column Percentages

	1973/4 PEP	1977/9 CRE	1984/5 PSI
Sales Rep (male)			
No discrimination	60	29	52
Discrimination v. black	32	65	38
Discrimination v. white	8	6	10
No. of vacancies covered by tests	66	23	99
Secretary (female)			
No discrimination	79	60	60
Discrimination v. black	19	35	33
Discrimination v. white	2	5	6
No. of vacancies covered by tests	36	20	89
Junior Clerk (female)			
No discrimination	56	47	51
Discrimination v. black	33	44	44
Discrimination v. white	11	9	5
No. of vacancies covered by tests	36	16	41
Skilled Manual (male)			
No discrimination	76	n.a.	70
Discrimination v. black	22	n.a.	27
Discrimination v. white	2	n.a.	3
No. of vacancies covered by tests	65	n.a.	68

Note: The percentages for the 1977/79 and 1984/5 studies are
calculated using the paired test model. See text for explanation.

proportion of employers discriminating against the black applicant, however, varies considerably. For the comparison group of jobs, the level is 30 per cent for the PEP study in 1973/4, 49 per cent for the Nottingham CRC study in 1977/9, and 37 per cent in the 1984/5 study.

It is important to remember that the date is not the only difference between the three studies: the PEP work covered six towns and cities (London, the West Midlands and the North West region were, however, all represented among them), the CRC study was confined to Nottingham, while our latest project covered only London, Birmingham and Manchester. There were also differences of detail in the execution of the tests: for instance, the Nottingham study did not treat application forms as positive responses, and this would tend to produce a slightly higher figure for the level of discrimination because employers are less likely to discriminate when sending out application forms than when offering interviews immediately. We should not, therefore, attempt a detailed speculative explanation for the fact that the overall level of discrimination found in this study is lower than that found in 1977/9 while it is higher than that found in 1973/4. However, we can be sure that there is no evidence here to suggest that racial discrimination in job recruitment has fallen over the period covered by these studies.

The best comparisons are those for the individual job types shown in Table 9. For the secretary and the female junior clerk the level of discrimination found in this study and in the 1977/9 study are remarkably similar, and are higher than those found in 1973/4. For the sales representative, the level found in the present study is somewhat higher than in 1973/4, but much lower than in the intervening study. For the skilled manual jobs - for which there were no corresponding tests in Nottingham - the level of discrimination is again slightly higher now than in 1973/4. Overall, the increase in the level of discrimination between 1973/4 and 1984/5 is not statistically significant - in other words it could be the result of random variations within the tests.

The changed job market
It is important to remember that since the 1973/4 study there has been a massive change in the job market in this country. Unemployment has risen and finding work has become more difficult. Since 1974 the official unemployment rate has grown from less than 3 per cent to more than 13 per cent(3). The burden has fallen more heavily on black people than on white people: results from the 1984 Labour Force Survey show that among blacks the proportion of economically active people who are unemployed is almost twice as high as it is among whites(4).

28

The recession has had a particularly hard impact on minority racial groups for a number of reasons. Black workers are disproportionately represented in the geographical areas and industrial sectors that have experienced the worst effects of the economic contraction. But also, as this study confirms, black people who are already suffering the consequences of these economic disadvantages face a further block to getting a job: substantial racial discrimination.

On average there are now many more job-seekers competing for each vacancy, and in this harsher job market one might expect that racial discrimination would have become more common. When recruiting staff an employer now has more opportunity to discriminate because the number of white applicants from which to choose is greater, and some employers might also be more inclined to discriminate during a job shortage because they hold the racialist view that white applicants are more 'deserving' than black applicants. The fact that there has been no change in the level of discrimination could therefore be seen as an encouraging sign; in other words, it could be argued that things mights have been worse. But this argument is only of value as speculation about employers' fundamental disposition to discriminate, outside the specific circumstances in which they make their decisions; we cannot measure this, and from our own tests we are unable to draw firm conclusions about any relationship between local unemployment levels and the extent of racial discrimination. And it would be small comfort to black British job-seekers, already having to contend with constricted job markets, to be advised that racial discrimination is only as bad as it used to be. The brutal fact is that, despite the law, direct discrimination persists as an additional and powerful impediment to any economic progress by blacks.

V Conclusions

Last year PSI published the report of its most recent survey of the circumstances of the British black population(5). In it we described in some detail the position that workers of Asian and West Indian ethnic origin occupy in the labour market, and how that has changed over the 1970s and early 1980s. Based on a nationwide interview survey of 5000 black adults and 2300 white adults in 1982, the report showed that both Asians and West Indians are found in jobs that are lower down the occupational ladder than whites, and are also more likely to be unemployed. Figure 1 gives an impression of the inequalities between whites and blacks. The study also showed that there had been very little change over the period 1974-1982 in the types of jobs in which blacks were found: this was demonstrated by reference to PSI's previous national survey and by examining the job histories of those interviewed in 1982.

In that report we suggested that, despite the Race Relations Act, continuing racial discrimination at the point of recruitment was an important factor in perpetuating this state of affairs. The most up-to-date direct evidence for this was the Nottingham study conducted between 1977 and 1979, and we were therefore cautious in our assertions about the actual level of discrimination: most of the work in Nottingham had been done only a year or two after the last Race Relations Act, and this had been in force for five years by the time of our survey in 1982 (the 1976 Race Relations Act became fully operative in June 1977). We were at pains to point out that the survey provided no new direct evidence of racial discrimination, despite that fact that it showed the continuing and in some ways worsening overall disadvantage of black people in the job market.

The results of the tests reported here show that racial discrimination has indeed continued to have a great impact on the employment opportunities of black people. We can summarise the findings in the following way:

30

(1)   In every job category and in all three cities we find substantial discrimination against the black applicants. The white applicant is over a third more likely to receive a positive response from the employer than are either of the black applicants. At least a third of the employers recruiting people to the jobs covered in this study discriminate against Asian applicants or West Indian applicants or both. We should emphasize here that this study aims to provide a minimum estimate of the extent of discrimination: the actual level is likely to be higher than that reported here.

(2)   There are no systematic differences between the overall levels of discrimination faced by Asian and West Indian applicants; this is also the case within each job category.

(3)   Although there are interesting differences between the results for the different job types, and between the results in the three areas, all are within the range one would expect to find as a result of random variation in a set of tests of this size, and none of the variations are consistent. This means we cannot point to any of the job types or areas as significant exceptions to the general findings on the level of discrimination.

(4)   Comparisons between this and previous studies show no evidence of a decrease in the extent of racial discrimination over the past decade. The levels of discrimination found in this study are in fact higher than those found in the PEP study of 1973/4, but the differences are not statistically significant.

The annual extent of discrimination

We have shown the results of these tests as proportions of applicants meeting discrimination and proportions of employers discriminating. Each time an employer makes an unfair choice because of the race of the applicant, he or she is breaking the law. How often does this happen every year in Britain? The answer to that question is impossible to give in exact terms, partly because our test results are very likely to be underestimates of the true extent of discrimination, but also because we do not have the necessary information about the number of vacancies for which black applicants compete with whites annually. But even a conservative estimate would put the figure at tens of thousands of acts of racial discrimination in job recruitment every year.

31

It should be noted that in the normal course of events a black applicant who is discriminated against would have no evidence to suggest that it had happened. In the majority of cases of discrimination in our tests a polite letter of refusal was sent to the victim, often 'explaining' that other applicants were better qualified and even in some cases wishing the applicant well in his or her search for a job. The applicant would have no reason to suspect he or she was a victim of racial discrimination and even if there was such a suspicion, there would be no immediately available evidence to support it. The individual illegal act of discrimination is often invisible to the victim.

Racial discrimination and the law

A major reason for the persistence of discrimination must be that an individual employer is very unlikely to be caught doing it. It seems that a proportion of decision-makers have a propensity to discriminate when selecting employees, either because of their own racialist attitudes or because they see it as expedient for the business. For many of them the fact that discrimination is illegal does not make the avoidance of discrimination a moral imperative. They continue to discriminate because there is only a minimal risk of detection. The legislation may originally have had an effect as a moral declaration but by now it can have no additional effect of that kind.

The law can be criticised for 'having few teeth' when dealing with cases that do come to light, and for the difficulties that face individual victims when pursuing their cases through the Tribunals or Courts; yet the heart of the problem is that employers know that cases rarely get as far as legal action because the victim is very unlikely to be aware that he or she has been discriminated against. In this field, as in others, the likelihood of detection is at least as important as the severity of penalty.

Individual court actions are not the only available method of enforcement of the law against racial discrimination. The Commission of Racial Equality has powers to mount investigations into the policies and practices of employers (and other organisations) to determine whether they have discriminated on racial grounds; with such systematic investigations it is possible to see what the individual victim cannot see - the employer's recruitment practice as a whole, and its consequences. This more strategic approach might therefore be justifiably expected to have a more powerful deterrent effect, if it were pursued on a sufficient scale. If an employer is (or has been) discriminating, this fact is unlikely to escape the close scrutiny that is possible under these provisions of the Race Relations Act. But scale is, of course, the problem. With the resources of the CRE at their present level the annual number of these investigations is bound to be small, so they are unlikely to have much of an impact on an employer's impression that discrimination is easy to get away with.

This argument leads us to conclude that if the law against racial discrimination is to have an increased impact on the actual extent of discrimination, then it must be through the deterrent effect of systematic and strategic investigations on a greater scale than at present and of legal actions stemming from them.

We have a law against racial discrimination not only to condemn but also to try to eradicate it. We can see from the research reported here that there has been no reduction in the extent of discrimination over the last decade, and it has been demonstrated elsewhere that the inequalities that result from this discrimination have become entrenched in British society. The choice is therefore plain: we can keep the Race Relations Act as a fine expression of what is right and what is wrong, while a substantial proportion of employers continue to hire people on the basis of their skin colour; or we can use the Act to try to stop discrimination, by a legal strategy that involves scrutinising a sufficient number of employers to make it a real deterrent.

Figure 1   The jobs of the three ethnic groups

Base: All economically active

Source: 1982 PSI Survey

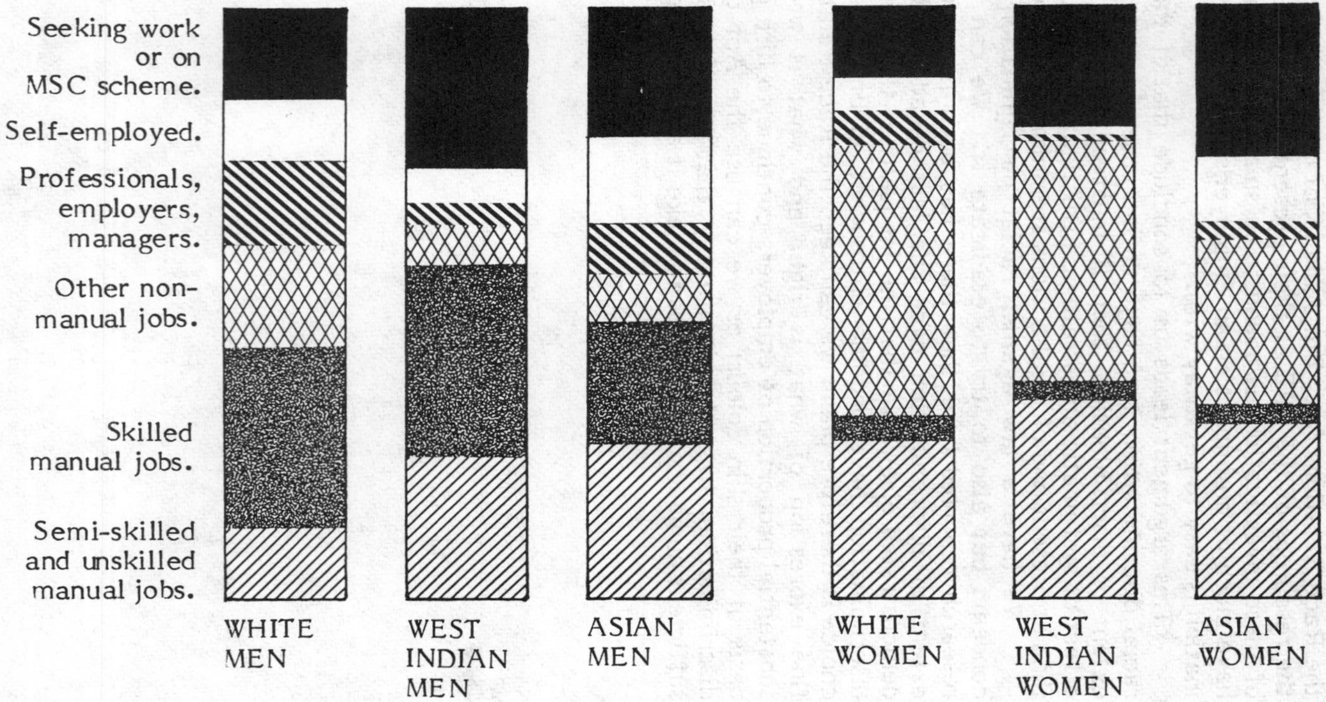

Seeking work or on MSC scheme.

Self-employed.

Professionals, employers, managers.

Other non-manual jobs.

Skilled manual jobs.

Semi-skilled and unskilled manual jobs.

WHITE MEN

WEST INDIAN MEN

ASIAN MEN

WHITE WOMEN

WEST INDIAN WOMEN

ASIAN WOMEN

REFERENCES

(1)   Neil McIntosh and David J. Smith, The Extent of Racial Discrimination, PEP Broadsheet No. 547, (London: PEP, 1974).

(2)   Jim Hubbuck and Simon Carter, Half a Chance? A report on job discrimination against young blacks in Nottingham, Commission for Racial Equality, (London: 1980).

(3)   Department of Employment Gazette, HMSO.

(4)   Written answer to parliamentary question. Commons Hansard, 8 July 1985, Written Answers, col.326.

(5)   Colin Brown, Black and White Britain: the third PSI Survey, Heinemann Educational Books (London: 1984).

The success rate of the three basic letter formats was checked to ensure that they could not have been a source of bias. It was found that 70 per cent of the letters sent out in each format had received positive responses.   Furthermore, equal numbers of each letter type had been sent for each of the three applicants.   It was therefore impossible that the variation between the basic letter types could have biased the test results.

We show below the standard texts of four batches of letters: the first is for the secretarial jobs, the second for the sales representative jobs, the third for the clerical jobs, and the fourth for the office junior jobs. In each batch the first letter was on a small sheet of tinted writing paper, the second on a slightly larger sheet of a different colour and the third on white A4 paper. The typefaces were also different, although we do not reproduce them here.

The three applicants' letter types were rotated between each vacancy; the details of the early schooling overseas for the West Indian applicant were of course only included in the appropriate letter.

The details of the applicant's most recent job, the name of the newspaper that carried the advertisement and other minor details were added as appropriate for each vacancy.

Dear .....

With reference to your advertisement in the ..... of ..... for the post of ....., I should like to be considered for the vacancy.

I received my secondary education in Coventry where I passed five GCEs at O-level and two at A-level. My O-level subjects were English Literature and English Language, History, Geography and Mathematics. My A-levels were in English and History, in both of which I gained Grade D. After leaving school I attended technical college where I did a two-year full-time business course. My typing speed is 60 wpm and my shorthand is 110 wpm. I also have the RSA Shorthand Typists' Certificate, Stage II.

My first job after leaving college was with a firm of architects where I worked for two of the junior partners. I saw to their correspondence, typed specifications and handled telephone calls from clients and construction personnel. My second job was as secretary to the director of a dye company and my duties there included audio-typing, organising meetings and making travel arrangements. In 1981 I took up my present position as .....

I am now 28 years old and am married. I hope my qualifications will enable me to obtain an interview.

Yours .....

(Mrs) Jean Miller

SECRETARIAL VACANCY - LETTER B

Dear .....

I am writing in reply to your advertisement of ..... in ..... for the position of ..... for which I feel I am suitably qualified. I am at present employed as .....

I am 29 years old and have been married for two years. I came to the UK in 1967 after completing my primary schooling in Jamaica. I attended secondary school in Dudley, which I left when I was eighteen with five 'O' levels, including Maths and English, and two Grade Ds at 'A' level (in English and General Studies). I spent the next year at a secretarial college where I attained speeds of 110 in shorthand and 50 in typing.

I took my present job two years ago after having worked first with a textile company, then as secretary to a regional sales executive. In the former job I learned a range of general office skills including telex and audio-typing and I was also involved in production and design documentation. This experience was useful when I moved to a busy sales office. There I was given more responsibilities, including delegating some of the work to junior staff and maintaining sales statistics.

Yours .....

Andrea Robinson

SECRETARIAL VACANCY - LETTER C

Dear .....

(JOB TITLE)

I should like to apply for the above position as advertised in .....

I am aged twenty-nine next month and at secondary school I passed G.C.E. Ordinary level in five subjects and obtained Ds at Advanced Level in English Literature and Economics. At Technical College I gained R.S.A. Intermediate Typewriting, and Pitman Shorthand Certificates for 120 w.p.m.

After leaving college in 1974 I worked for the Assistant Sales Manager of a well-known Solihull manufacturing firm as a junior shorthand-typist. It was an interesting and varied job but in June 1976 I applied for the position of audio-secretary at a large estate agents' where I was dealing with clients both personally and over the telephone. I was later promoted to assistant office manager. Since my marriage in August 1980 I have been resident in Birmingham and working as .....

I should be very pleased to come for an interview at any time suitable to you.

Yours .....

<u>Indira Malhotra</u> (Mrs.)

39

SALES VACANCY - LETTER A

Dear .....

With reference to your advertisement in the ..... of ..... for the post of ....., I should like to apply for the vacancy.

I have been permanently resident in England since 1962 when my parents came to this country from Jamaica. I left school with six 'O' levels - Maths and English Language (both Grade B), Biology (C), History (C), Commerce (C) and Art (C). I then went on to complete a one-year course in Business Studies at a technical college.

My first job was with a confectionery manufacturer where I worked first in dispatch and then as a van salesman. I later joined the sales force of a company which manufactured surgical dressings, to begin with as a correspondence sales clerk and later as a sales representative for the Hospital Division (West Midlands Region). In early 1981 I took up my present position selling .....

At various times I have covered both the East and West Midlands territories. I am now 29 years of age and married with one child. I hope my qualifications will enable me to obtain an interview.

Yours .....

Winston Robinson

SALES VACANCY - LETTER B

Dear .....

I am writing in reply to your advertisement of ..... in the ..... for a
....., for which I feel I am suitably qualified. I am at present
employed as a member of the sales team of a .....

I am twenty-eight years old, married, with two children. I have
Ordinary Level passes in:

English Language,	Grade B	Principles of Accounts,	Grade C
English Literature	" C	Mathematics	" B
Religious Studies	" C	Integrated Science	" C

After I completed my secondary education I did not go straight to
work but to a further education college to take a course in
Commerce for the following year. I then went on to work in an
insurance company in a clerical capacity.

I took up my present job towards the end of 1980 after having spent
a number of years as a salesman, first with a television rental
company and then selling to interior decorators and do-it-yourself
shops for a paints firm.

I should naturally be happy to attend an interview at any time this
is convenient to you.

Yours .....

(Satish Malhotra)

41

SALES VACANCY - LETTER C

Dear .....

(JOB TITLE)

I should like to apply for the above position as advertised in ..... I shall be thirty next month and am married with a child aged two.

Having gained six G.C.E. 'O' level passes at the secondary school I attended in Dudley, I went on to a local college of technology to study Business Administration for a year. My first job after completing this course was as a clerk in the Accounts and subsequently the Sales Department of a company which manufactured packaging materials. I later became a trainee salesman and stayed with the company for a period of three years in all. I was next employed by a national manufacturer of office equipment with a sales territory based on the Midlands (East and West).

My present job, which I have held for the past three years, is as a representative centred on the West Midlands area for a well-known .....

I am available to attend for interview at any time suitable to you and I look forward to your reply.

Yours .....

Brian Miller

CLERICAL VACANCY - LETTER A

Dear .....

I write with reference to your advertisement in the ..... of ..... for a ..... I should like to apply for the vacancy.

I am thirty years of age. I left school at the age of sixteen with five O-levels which included Maths and English Language. I then went on to complete a one-year course in Business Studies at a technical college.

I started work as an office junior in the West Midlands head-quarters of a leading brewery. The company sent me on day release to learn typing and during the three years I spent in this job I performed a wide variety of office duties. In 1973 I obtained a post as clerk-typist with an export company and four years ago moved to my present position as .....

I hope these qualifications will lead to an interview for the vacancy. I am available to come at any time you find convenient.

Yours .....

(Mrs) Indira Malhotra

CLERICAL VACANCY - LETTER B

Dear .....

I should like to be considered for the vacancy for a ..... in today's ..... I shall be aged 31 next month and I am currently employed as a ..... in the offices of a leading department store in the city centre where I have worked since 1979.

At secondary school I obtained five Ordinary Level passes (in History, Geography, Commerce, English and Mathematics). After completing my secondary education I did not go straight to work but to a further education college to take a course in Business Administration for the following year. My first job at the age of 17 was as a junior office assistant in a local government department. I stayed in this job for three years or so and during that time attended a typing course at evening school.

I then moved to a job in the general office of a large manufacturing company, at first as a filing clerk, then as an assistant in the Wages Section, until obtaining my present position.

I can come for interview at any time, if, as I hope, this outline of my work experience to date qualifies me for consideration for the vacancy.

Yours .....

Jean Miller

CLERICAL VACANCY - LETTER C

Dear .....

(JOB TITLE)

I would like to apply for the above vacancy which I saw advertised in .....

My family came to this country from Jamaica in 1958. I attended primary and secondary schools in Wolverhampton and gained G.C.E. 'O' levels in five subjects. These included Commercial Studies as well as English Language and Mathematics and I was accepted by my local college of technology to study Commerce for a year after leaving school.

My first job after completing this course was as a junior in the Accounts Department of a publishing firm. I was there for almost $3\frac{1}{2}$ years. When my family moved to Birmingham I obtained a position as clerk/typist in the Contracts Department of a large company dealing with electrical goods. I stayed with this company for just under six years but have now been nearly four years in my present position as a ..... with a ..... I am now 30 years old.

I look forward to hearing from you and would be glad to attend for interview whenever it would be suitable from your point of view.

Yours .....

<u>Andrea Robinson</u> (Mrs.)

OFFICE JUNIOR VACANCY - LETTER A

Dear .....

I am writing in reply to your advertisement of ..... in ..... for a .....
I should like to apply for the vacancy. I am 19 years old and came
to the West Midlands from Jamaica in 1968, and I have six GCE O-
levels. These are: Maths and English Language (both Grade B),
Biology (C), History (C), Commerce (C) and Art (C). I

I left school in June 1980 and I am now working as a ..... in a well-
known .....

I should like an opportunity to do more work in ..... and am
therefore very interested in your vacancy. I can come for
interview at any time.

Yours .....

Andrea Robinson

OFFICE JUNIOR VACANCY - LETTER B

Dear .....

I should like to apply for the vacancy of ..... which you advertised in .....

I shall be nineteen next month. I left school with Ordinary Level passes in:

English Language,	Grade B	Principles of Accounts,	Grade C
English Literature	" C	Mathematics	" B
Religious Studies	" C	Integrated Science	" C

Since then I have been working in ..... where I have been .....

I should be pleased to come for an interview at any time suitable to you.

Yours .....

Indira Malhotra (Miss)

OFFICE JUNIOR VACANCY - LETTER C

Dear .....

(JOB TITLE)

I would like to apply for the above position as advertised in .....

I left school in 1980 when I was sixteen and worked in a ..... in Coventry as a ..... I left this job in ..... when my parents moved back to Birmingham.

At school I obtained 6 GCE passes. My subjects were Chemistry, English Language, Computing Studies, Mathematics, Modern British Economy and Music. My grades were, respectively, C, B, C, B, C and C.

I am available to attend for interview at any time you find convenient.

Yours .....

(Jean Miller)

APPENDIX II EXAMPLES OF DISCRIMINATION: REPLIES FROM EMPLOYERS

We show four sets of replies here. They are not chosen to be representative of all the employers' replies, but to demonstrate the fact that victims of discrimination are unlikely to be aware of what has happened. In each case the rejection letters are polite and give no indication that the applicant has been rejected on the basis of ethnic origin.

Example 1:   An office supplies firm

The reply to the white applicant:

Dear Sir,

Thank you for your recent application for the position of Sales Representative with this Company.

Interviews will be held at .... Birmingham on .... Will you please attend at 2.00 p.m.

Please ask for .... on arrival.

Yours faithfully ......

The reply to the Asian and West Indian applicants:

Dear Sir/Madam,

Sales Representative

Thank you for your recent application for the above situation.

We regret to inform you that on this occasion your application for interview was not successful. However, we would like to thank you for the interest you have shown in our Company and wish you every success in your future endeavours.

Yours faithfully ......

Example 2: A building supplies firm

The reply to the white applicant (delivered by hand):

Dear Miss Miller,

Thank you for your recent letter concerning the position here as an 'office clerk'. Your application is of interest to us and I would be grateful if you could contact me on (number) as soon as possible to arrange an interview.

Looking forward to hearing from you, I remain,

Yours sincerely ......

The reply to the West Indian applicant (the Asian applicant received the same letter):

Dear Miss Robinson,

Further to your recent application as an 'Office Clerk' with this company, I must advise you that unfortunately, you have not been selected for the position.

May I take this opportunity to thank you for your interest, and wish you every success with your future career.

Yours sincerely ......

Example 3: A motor parts manufacturer

Some rejection letters were particularly polite and encouraging, as this example shows. The black applicants were told that their details would be kept for future reference, in case other vacancies arose.

The reply to the white applicant:

> Dear Mr. Miller,
>
> Further to your recent application for the position of Sales Representative, I have arranged an interview for you at 2.15 pm on .... at ....
>
> If this time is not convenient, please contact myself or ...., otherwise I will look forward to meeting you at the aforementioned time.
>
> Yours sincerely ......

The reply to the Asian applicant (the West Indian applicant received the same letter):

> Dear Mr. Malhotra,
>
> Thank you for your recent letter of application in response to our advertisements for Area Sales Representatives.
>
> Unfortunately, I must advise you that, on this occasion, you have been unsuccessful; however, further expansion is planned for our Sales Force during the course of 1984, and I intend to retain your details on file, and should a similar vacancy arise in the future, I shall contact you again.
>
> May I take this opportunity to thank you for your interest in our Company.
>
> Yours sincerely ......

Example 4: A company in the finance sector

This was a case in which the employer did keep the details for later reference, but then contacted only the white applicant when another vacancy arose.

The reply to all three applicants (following a holding letter):

> Dear Mrs. .....
>
> Further to Mr. .....'s letter of .... I write to advise you that the advertised position has now been filled.
>
> I would take this opportunity of thanking you for your interest and trust that you will find suitable employment in the near future.
>
> Yours sincerely ......

This letter was sent to the white applicant four days later:

> Dear Mrs. Miller,
>
> Further to my letter of ...... and due to unforeseen circum-stances a vacancy still in fact exists at this office.
>
> If therefore you still wish to be considered for the previously advertised vacancy perhaps you would kindly telephone me to arrange a mutually convenient appointment. On the assumption that you do wish to proceed further with this matter I enclose herewith an Application for Employment Form which should be completed in your own handwriting and brought with you to the interview.
>
> Yours sincerely ......

APPENDIX III STATISTICAL TESTS

In this report we make a number of comparisons of test results: between ethnic groups, between job types, between men and women, between age groups, between areas, and between studies carried out at different times. In each case we have applied the chi-squared test to indicate whether the differences shown up by the comparison are likely to have occured as a result of random variation.

The chi-squared test for the comparisons between the ethnic groups were carried out using the raw figures from Tables 3, 5 and 7. For all the other comparisons the chi-squared tests were carried out using the paired-test model as described in the text and as shown in Tables 8 and 9. Thus the variable used in the statistical comparison between the success of the different ethnic groups had two values -

(1)   Positive outcome of application
(2)   Negative outcome of application

- while the variable used in the statistical comparison between the levels of discrimination of the different jobs, sex and age groups, areas and years had three values -

(1)   No discrimination
(2)   Discrimination against black applicant
(3)   Discrimination against white applicant.

For each of the latter type of chi-squared test the calculations were carried out for the levels of discrimination against the Asian and West Indian applicants separately as well as jointly.

As explained in the text, in all cases except one the relationships classed as statistically significant had a chi-squared value with a probability of less than 0.01 (the exception had a probability of less than 0.05; see page 19). The overall difference between the success rates of black and white applicants was significant at the 0.001 level. All of the relationships classed as not statistically significant had a chi-squared value with a probability of more than 0.05.

APPENDIX IV PREVIOUS DISCRIMINATION TEST STUDIES

Country & Date of Study	Researchers	Description
England 1966-67	W.W.Daniel, PEP	Test applications made to landlords, accommodation bureaux and estate agents; and to employers who had, on the evidence of survey informants, committed previous acts of discrimination. Widespread discrimination was found in all these fields. See W.W. Daniel, <u>Racial Discrimination in England</u>, Penguin Books (Harmondsworth: 1968) and <u>Racial Discrimination</u>, Political and Economic Planning/Research Services Ltd (London: 1967)
England 1969	Roger Jowell and Patricia Prescott-Clarke, Social & Community Planning Research	Postal applications to employees advertising non-manual job vacancies. Found a significant extent of racial discrimination, particularly against Asians. See R. Jowell and P. Prescott-Clarke, 'Racial Discrimination and white-collar workers in Britain', in <u>Race</u>, Vol.XI, No.4, April 1970.

England   Neil McIntosh
1973-74   & David J. Smith   Actor and postal application to em-
          P.E.P.   ployers, landlords, accom-modation
                                 agencies and estate agents. Found
                                 extensive   discrimination   against
                                 black applicants, particularly in em-
                                 ployment recruitment (see text of
                                 this report). See N. McIntosh and
                                 D.J. Smith, The Extent of Racial
                                 Discrimination, PEP Broadsheet No.
                                 547 (London: PEP, 1974).

Holland   Frank Bovenkerk,
1976   University of Utrecht
                                 Postal and telephone applications
                                 for   manual   and   non-manual
                                 vacancies in Amsterdam. Responses
                                 to Dutch, Surinamese and Spanish
                                 applicants   showed   discrimination
                                 against the minority applicants. See
                                 Frank Bovenkerk and Elsbeth Breu-
                                 ning-van Leeuwen, 'Rasdiscriminatie
                                 en rasvooroordeel op de Amsterda-
                                 mse arbeidsmarkt', in F. Bovenkerk
                                 (ed), Omdat zij anders zijn: Pat-
                                 ronen   van   rasdiscriminatie   in
                                 Nederland,   Boom   Meppel
                                 (Amsterdam: 1978).

England   Michael Firth,
1977-78   Victoria University   Postal applications to advertising
          of New Zealand   jobs in the finance sector. Found
                                 some discrimination against foreign
                                 whites and considerable discrimin-
                                 ation against non-whites. See M.
                                 Firth, 'Racial Discrimination in the
                                 British Job Market', in Industrial &
                                 Labor Relations Review, Vol. 34,
                                 No.2, Jan. 1981.

USA   Jerry Newman,
1977   State University
          of New York,   Unsolicited postal applications to
          Buffalo   employers with affirmative action
                                 plans. Complex findings showing an

overall bias in favour of black applicants in larger firms and in favour of white applicants in the smaller firms. See Jerry M. Newman, 'Discrimination in Recruitment: An Empirical Analysis', in Industrial and Labor Relations Review, Vol. 32, No.1, October 1978.

England   Jim Hubbuck
1977-79   & Simon Carter
           Nottingham CRC   Postal applications to employers advertising non-manual vacancies. Found extensive discrimination against black applicants (see text of this report). See J. Hubbuck and S. Carter, Half a Chance? A report on job discrimination against young blacks in Nottingham, CRE, (London: 1980).

Australia Peter Riach
1984-   Monash University   Study of race and sex discrimination in progress.